I love that you're my

Grandpa

because

Copyright © 2018 River Breeze Press
All rights reserved. This book or any portion thereof
may not be reproduced or used in any manner whatsoever without the express written permission of the publisher.

I Love You Because Books
www.riverbreezepress.com

To Grandpa

Love, _____

Date: _____

The best thing about you is your

_____

Thank you for being patient with me when

_____

You are better than a

_____

You should win the grand prize for

_____

You make me feel special when

_____

Grandpa, I love you more than

_____

I love when you tell me about

_____

I love when we

_____

together

You taught me how to

_____

I know you love me because

_____

I wish I could

_____

as well as you do

Grandpa, I love that we have the same

_____

You should be the king of

_____

You have an amazing talent for

_____

Grandpa, you make me laugh when you

_____

I wish I had more time to

_____

with you

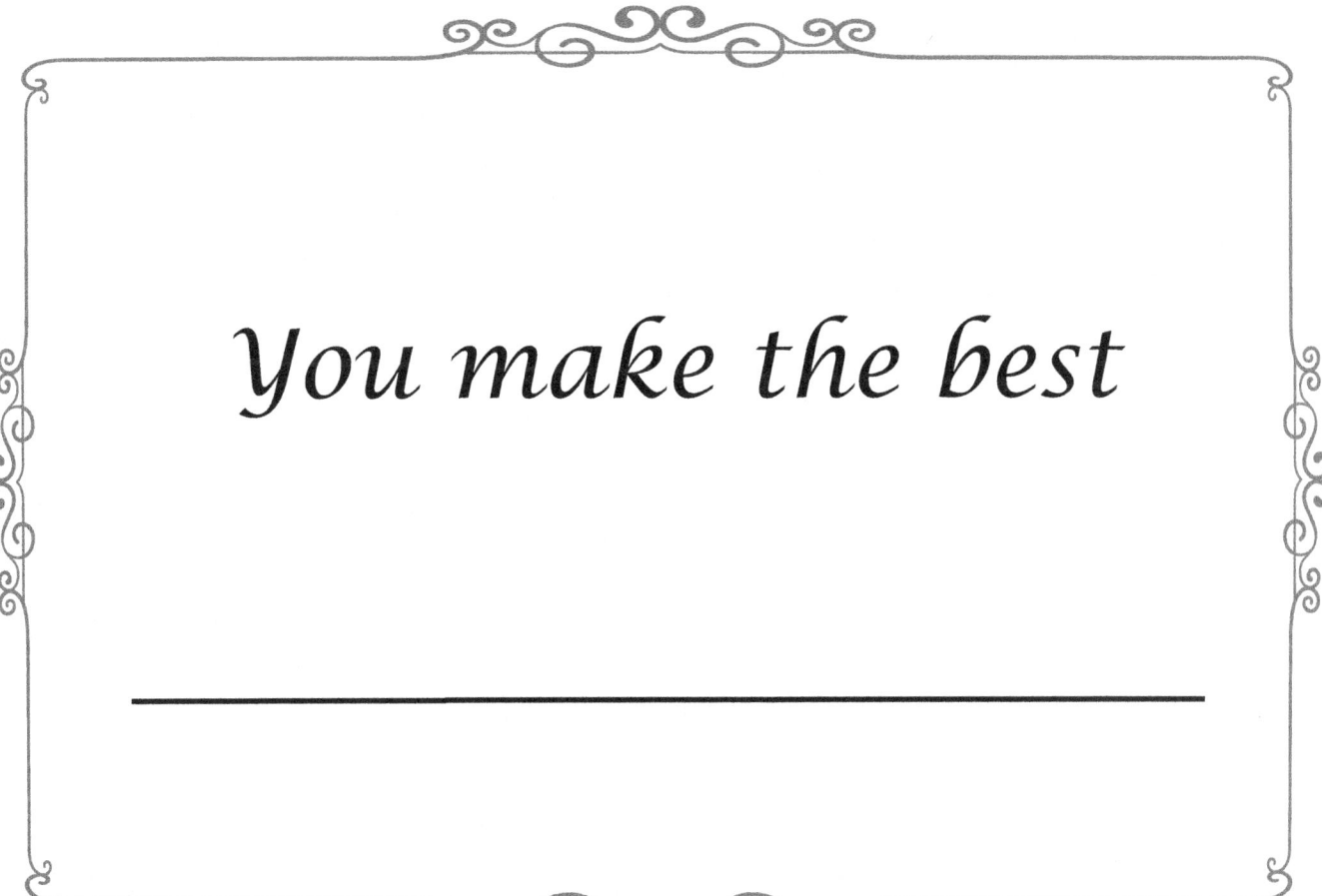

You make the best

_____

If I could give you anything it would be

_____

I would love to go

_____

with you

You are there for me when

_____

Grandpa, I love you because you are

_____

Made in the USA
Monee, IL
30 May 2021